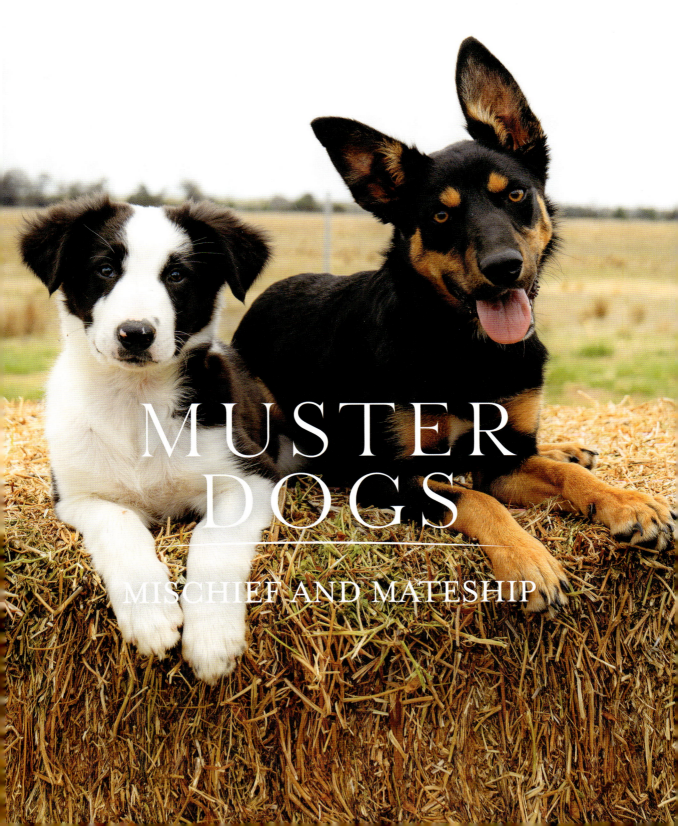

Melissa Spencer
Monica O'Brien
Michael Boughen

MUSTER DOGS

MISCHIEF AND MATESHIP

ABC
BOOKS

CONTENTS

Foreword by Lisa Millar.....................................9

Foreword by Frank Finger........................10

Introduction..15

1 Shaping Future Muster Dogs.................20

2 Preparing Puppies for Purpose............72

3 Muster Dogs in Action.........................110

4 Golden Oldies......................................170

Acknowledgements................................185

Locations...187

Photo Credits...187

About the Authors.................................189

Foreword by Lisa Millar

There was a moment in the second series of *Muster Dogs* when the camera captured our breeder, Carolyn Hudson, shedding a tear. She was preparing to say farewell to the litter of border collies she'd grown to love over the past three months. With her bare hands, she'd helped some of them into the world while their mother laboured, losing sleep as she waited to caress and check each pup as it tumbled into the birthing box. She'd cared for them, bathed them, run with them and talked to them. And now she was giving them to strangers. She was embarrassed our television audience would see her in this emotional state.

It was nothing to be ashamed of, I told her. In fact, her fragility on screen in that moment perfectly summed up the intensity of the relationship between these beautiful working dogs and their handlers. People on the land love their animals, and we were privileged to show our audiences that. Even though I was a kid from the country, I hadn't really known or understood the skill of true working dogs. It was an eye opener.

And what fun filming *Muster Dogs* has been. As puppies, they peed on our tripods, licked our cameras, chewed on microphones and wriggled like squids, testing our patience but always making us smile. And then, like butterflies emerging from a chrysalis, the pups' limbs grew, their ears cocked to attention, and we joined them on a journey of great importance. They shed their mischievousness and thrived under their meticulous trainers. And we were suddenly no longer the teachers, but the taught.

The dogs became the bearers of the message that work on the land could be done differently, more efficiently, in a more environmentally sound way. And these dogs, who'd become our mates, would lead the way.

Foreword by Frank Finger

Most of the photography in *Muster Dogs: Mischief and Mateship* was splendidly captured through the lens of Melissa Spencer's cameras. The images of pups and dogs at work and play are majestic. The book's title describes exactly what happened at my property 'Hillview' over the years. Growing up, we always had dogs around the homestead. These dogs were like Dolly Parton's coat: their own coats were of many colours, breed mixes unknown. They were dogs that would hide under the house and bite you as you walked up the steps. We had to jump up the stairs to avoid being bitten, but nothing was ever done about them. They just went back under the house to await their next victim.

Fast forward to 1996, we hosted a Neil and Helen McDonald working-dog-training and stock-handling school. This was the start of some very big changes at 'Hillview'. We went on to host their schools every year since, and, when demand was high, we would have multiple schools. We hosted their 39th last year.

I write this to demonstrate how important it is to learn how to learn and how important it is to get training in whatever it is you want to do or be. Nothing beats getting knowledge and skills from the right people. Dogs and people don't care what you know until they know you care. To get the best out of your working dogs, you have to show them heartfelt care and love, which brings me to the very successful ABC series. This program has given the participants, dog trainers, dog educators and dog breeders the chance to showcase our care and love for our dogs, our livestock and the rural industry, as well as show our pride and passion in what we do to help feed the world. I also hope the kindness that we have shown to our dogs has given other dogs a better life, and that *Mischief and Mateship* finds its way into the hearts and memories of its readers and onto coffee tables right across Australia, and maybe even around the world.

INTRODUCTION

Our country, Australia, is more than the rich foundation we have built our lives on, yet its landscape and terrain are the embodiment of what it is to be Australian. Our country is resilient and diverse, lush and arid, flat and mountainous.

And those qualities are reflected in and have shaped our First Nations people and every immigrant who has called this country home.

As we traverse our time on country, we seek out those companions that enrich the journey. Many of these comrades are human, but the most loyal enter our lives full of mischief, wide-eyed and spirited. They are an ally from dawn till dusk and a mate for life. They are our muster dogs, and as you explore this book in celebration of working dogs, their journeys of mischief to mateship will fill your cup with joy.

SHAPING FUTURE MUSTER DOGS

Our agricultural industry is essential to providing local and global food security, and it is a tough gig. Working on the land is physically and emotionally fatiguing and directly impacted by forces completely out of a grazier's control. The success or failure of a season is not only blowing in the changing winds, it can also be affected by pests and parasites – both biological and political – so when it comes to building a team to endure it with you, a loyal working dog is the first pick of most graziers seeking to improve their odds and secure success.

It's estimated that there are more than 270,000 working dogs kicking up dust as they race across paddocks around Australia. Everyone wants the Best Dog, and when it comes to picking one, genetics is the key.

Everyone is looking for a good dog, but then they get hung up on preferences and immediately start halving their chances on finding a good dog. People need to be open minded and stop worrying about breed, gender or colour, and choose a pup from a bloodline of dogs that has work attributes and traits that meet your needs and your working style — Neil McDonald

When it comes to pedigree bloodlines, our muster dogs are born with personalities that make them likeable and easy to bond with, as well as natural desire and instinct to stalk and herd stock, and physical strength, stamina and colouring, which allows them to work safely in Australian conditions.

Multiple seasons of *Muster Dogs* have proved that if you get the genetics right you're more than 50 per cent on track to having a great working dog. The rest comes down to the handler and their ability to be in tune with the stock and effectively communicate with the dog in a way that keeps it motivated, engaged and feeling appreciated.

SHAPING FUTURE MUSTER DOGS   **23**

FIRST MOMENTS

The mewling and puking sounds of newborn pups are phenomenally loud, given their tiny size. Nature truly is incredible and, as the mother licks her pups to life, literally awakening their senses to take their first breaths, the pups' desire to survive is immediately switched on. It is this desire to seek out food that is fundamental to their natural herding instinct – to work in a pack to stalk and hunt stock in order to eat and survive.

At this magical birth stage, steak is not what the puppies are seeking. They blindly wriggle across their mother's body and over their siblings seeking out milk. And for mothers with big litters, ensuring even distribution of the nutritious white gold is a fatiguing task. The pack rivalry begins, and a guiding human hand is often needed to separate the guzzling gutses from the runts to ensure even growth across the litter.

These gorgeous Australian border collie pups were bred by Mick and Carolyn Hudson and born to mother Debbie in the early hours of the morning. Debbie delivered a litter of ten lively puppies for series 2 of *Muster Dogs*.

Sweet dreams, little ones! Just a few days old and small enough to fit in your hands.

CLOCKWISE FROM TOP RIGHT: Muster Dog Indi; kelpies Shiny and Glimmer; Muster Dog Molly; and Muster Dog Snow.

Three-day-old kelpie pups from series 1 of *Muster Dogs*.

Kelpie pup Jean exploring her new surroundings.

Kelpie Gemma sits proudly with her litter of eleven pups.

MISCHIEF MAKERS

Watching puppies rumble and play is pure joy, except for when the object of their pouncing and gnawing is your shoe! The playtime stage is an exciting and expressive time, during which personality traits begin to emerge and puppies explore their surroundings. Discovering if a pup is a leader or follower, courageous or timid, mischievous or mindful helps the handler determine how the pup will emerge as a working dog. This is a time to observe what instincts come naturally and what areas might need to be worked on – whether it's confidence, encouragement or discipline.

The time they spend playing is thrilling and stimulating for pups as they use all their senses to engage with the environment and burn off energy, and it gives an early insight to their stamina and agility.

RIGHT: Muster Dog Lucky (right) was the chief mischief maker of the litter, proving that being deaf was no impediment to a life of adventure and play.

Whether you're a kelpie or a collie, gnawing on sticks and boots is pure pleasure — but not for those who own the shoes. These playful and mischievous dogs will turn anything they can get their paws on into the ultimate chew toy and take any opportunity for a game of tug-of-war.

These smiley pups — Muster Dog Pockets, Muster Dog Hudson, Solly and Muster Dog Chief, with their brother Bandit hiding in the back — are from the same litter and were bred by Mick and Carolyn Hudson for series 3. They look calm and composed now but the chance of capturing that moment of 'all eyes to the camera' was a billion to one, as they bounced out of the barrow seconds later.

SHAPING FUTURE MUSTER DOGS

Muster Dog Molly (left) was the smallest pup of the series 2 litter but that didn't stop her from having the confidence to team up during puppy playtime with her big brother Muster Dog Buddy (right), who was the largest pup of the litter.

THIS PAGE: For this energetic litter of Muster Dog kelpies, the best toys are the camera crew's technical equipment.

RIGHT: Kelpie Buffer primed for playtime, with a stance that exudes playful energy.

TOP: Border collie Belle embracing the simple joys, stick in mouth and ready for adventures.

LEFT: Muster Dog Indi (left) is not as thrilled as her best buddy, Bobby McGee (right), to be wearing Christmas antlers.

THIS PAGE: It's a big day for Muster Dog Indi: she's just had her first encounter with sheep.

SHAPING FUTURE MUSTER DOGS 43

CONNECTION AND CARE

Cuddling a puppy is never a chore. Their soft, fluffy cuteness and big-hearted infatuation and interest in you make these early months mutually rewarding. But this time is also the most important stage on the puppy's path to becoming a successful working dog.

This bonding time with a dog is programming it with desirable endorphins that it will associate with affection and reward from you. Each interaction hardwires the puppy to see you as the pack leader and the provider of food, which the pup knows naturally from birth that it needs to survive.

The play, handling and gentle discipline you provide at this time give the puppy the boundaries and scaffolding it needs to stay safe, feel emotionally confident and socialised, and fuels its desire to be with you, be loyal to you and ultimately be waiting with excited anticipation to receive commands from you.

RIGHT: Sunset snuggles! Carolyn Hudson and border collie Patch, gazing into each other's eyes.

Series experts and educators Helen McDonald (left) and Carolyn Hudson (right) bonding with their litters of puppies.

Mick Hudson, celebrated trialling champion and dog educator, enjoying precious moments with his litter of young pups before they go off to their new owners.

Blythe and Muster Dog Banksi, perfectly coordinated in matching yellow and bonding immediately.

Keri and Muster Dog Indi sharing a moment on the day Indi was delivered to Winton.

TOP AND RIGHT: Saying goodbye is always tough for breeders, but knowing their pups are going to a good home makes it easier. Muster Dog Hudson's collar is Marlene's favourite colour, purple.

BELOW: There's a lot of excitement when Muster Dog Pesto first meets Jack and his family.

The series 2 *Muster Dogs* litter, eagerly waiting for Carolyn to open the gate so they can begin their day's work.

BRINGING OUT THE NATURAL INSTINCT

By eight weeks of age the fit and healthy puppies have a self-confidence that needs to be stimulated and harnessed. If not, it can lead to less desirable habits focused on digging, destroying (everything not nailed down) and squabbling with litter mates. Introducing puppies to educated stock at this age excites the desire to herd in them, burns off physical and nervous energy, and is truly fascinating to watch.

Without any instruction at all, a well-bred pup, which has been nurtured and handled carefully, transitions from an easily distracted frolicker to a single-minded hunter.

RIGHT: Muster Dog Indi, fearlessly showing her mettle during her first encounter with sheep. That direct stare speaks volumes about her natural dominance.

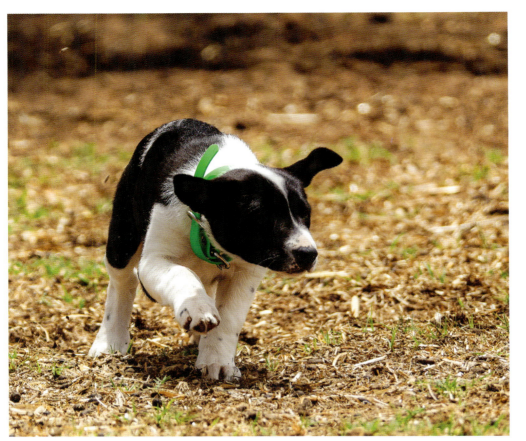

The first time a pup encounters stock gives trainers a sense of their dog's natural abilities. Muster Dog Pockets (left and below) shows confidence, calmly holding sheep against the fence, while Muster Dog Molly (right) exhibits remarkable calm and sensibility.

Young kelpie Mustang displays no fear or hesitation as this sheep leaps into the air — a promising glimpse of a dominant, natural working dog.

All these pups are showing innate herding ability, natural balance and a strong desire to work.

Clockwise from top far right: border collie Creedite; border collie Bandit; Muster Dog Pesto; Muster Dog Snow; and Muster Dog Buddy.

THIS PAGE: During their first look at stock, these pups show off natural style and eye. Clockwise from top right: kelpie Jean; border collie Heidi; and Muster Dog Banjo.

RIGHT: Muster Dog Banksi fearlessly approaches a sheep nose-to-nose, showing an eagerness to work.

ALL TUCKERED OUT

Living your best puppy life is such hard work, and going from full revs at playtime to deep snoring sleep takes all but a matter of seconds. If you could see their dreams, they would be filled with images of you and chewed shoes.

RIGHT: Muster Dog Chief, curled up at his carer Carolyn's feet after a long morning walk. These pups can, and will, nap anywhere!

It's tough being a pup! These border collie and kelpie puppies are all tuckered out after playing with their siblings, dreaming of tomorrow's adventures.

Clockwise from top right: Muster Dog Pockets; Muster Dog Banksi; kelpie Jungle; and Solly, Muster Dog Pockets and Muster Dog Chief.

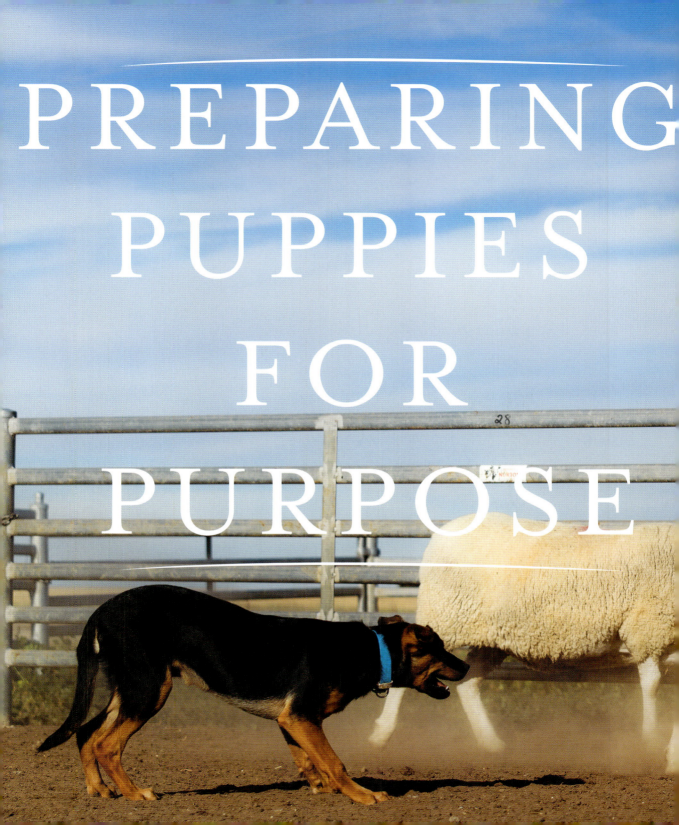

PREPARING PUPPIES FOR PURPOSE

Unconditional love is the lens our puppies see us through. They offer their devotion freely and want nothing more than to be by our sides and please us. A good trainer nurtures their pup's adoration by providing kindness and meaningful, focused engagement.

National dog trial champion and dog educator Mick Hudson believes that once you have this reciprocal bond established training can begin, utilising the key principles of Reward, Repetition and Reinforce. Every request or command needs to be verbally labelled with a consistent word, sound or gesture. When the dog actions that command you need to reinforce the labelling of it, and when the dog performs the task, you reward it with the acknowledgement and affection that it's been seeking. It's this desire to feel the endorphins of the reward that will motivate the later adult dog to show up for work – to get out of bed on a blisteringly hot day and mob up the cattle or wade through the winter grass and mud to shift the sheep.

LEFT: Muster Dog Banjo's ears are alert and focused, signalling his readiness to tackle the day's work.

PREPARING PUPPIES FOR PURPOSE

Best buddies Bobby McGee (left) and Muster Dog Indi (right) sit side by side, eagerly awaiting their next adventure.

Muster Dog Pockets springs into the air with pure joy, leaping out of the water trough in a spirited display of enthusiasm.

LEARNING THE ROPES

Respectful focus goes both ways when it comes to dog (and human) training. If the pup knows you are focused and in tune with it, the pup will reward your attention by doing what you request. In order to progress through the weeks and months of training, it's important to be in the right mindset and to clear the lines of communication between you and the pup.

If a pup suspects you're not in the zone for building the working relationship together, it will get distracted and give in to the overwhelming temptation to sniff! Success at this stage is reaching a state of mutual connection where the pup is by your side, tuned to you and on a loose lead.

LEFT: Eyes locked and grinning widely, Muster Dog Banjo knows how to melt hearts.

PREPARING PUPPIES FOR PURPOSE

ABOVE: Series 1 winner Frank Finger leads Muster Dog Annie on a loose lead in the early stages of training.

ABOVE: Renowned dog trainer Neil McDonald patiently coaches kelpie pup Connie during a training session, expertly employing a rope to teach essential skills and commands.

LEFT: Border collie Maggie May focuses intently as she learns the crucial skill of sitting calmly while working with stock.

RIGHT: Kelpie Jack and Muster Dog Pockets learning to stay put on a hay bale. While they appear calm and obedient here, seconds later they were off and running.

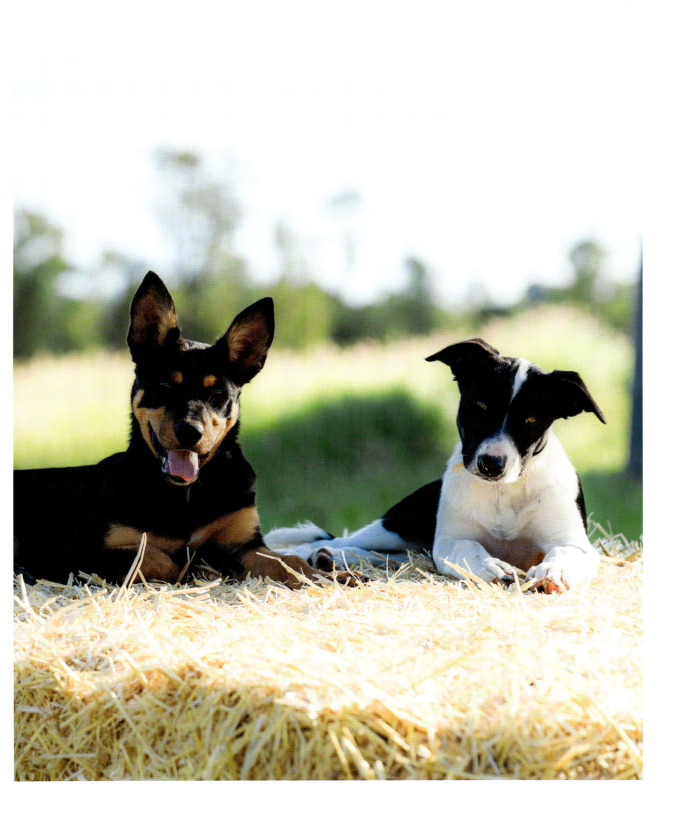

A working dog has to learn how to jump up on two- and four-wheelers and patiently await commands.

Clockwise from top right: Muster Dog Gossip practises her balance while checking out cattle in the Pilbara; four-month-old Muster Dog Annie waits for a signal from Frank; and Muster Dog Chief is a cheeky and enthusiastic student.

83

PART OF THE PACK

After months of feeling like the centre of your universe, and once it has enough manners to not irritate the other dogs in the family, your pup is ready to join the pack, where you will no longer be its greatest influence. Like a child starting school, bad habits either get knocked out of it or reinforced, and a new period of mischief making begins.

LEFT: Kelpie Indi, Muster Dog Chief, kelpie Reggie and kelpie Captain: a dream team.

PREPARING PUPPIES FOR PURPOSE

It's important for every young pup to be part of a team.

BLUETOOTH AND BONDING

There is nothing more affirming than eye contact, a connection that we as humans are rapidly losing in this new digital world we operate in. Rarely lifting our eyes from our screens and communicating in text and acronyms are impacting our ability to read the nuanced emotions of those we engage with.

When bonding with your pup and introducing recall and commands, having eye contact is essential. Your reward for that exchange is seeing the sparkle in your dog's eyes as it takes you in with singular focus, reading your energy and anticipating your command.

Quality working dogs use this same intuition to seek out the eye of the stock, read its intention and spring into action in response.

LEFT: Nose-to-nose and heart-to-heart, Muster Dog Chief and Nathan are totally in sync!

PREPARING PUPPIES FOR PURPOSE **89**

Muster Dog Indi joyfully jumps up to Steve, their smiles lighting up the photo.

Jack and Muster Dog Pesto delighting in a tummy rub, while she learns not to be a squid in his arms.

These dogs and their handlers are holding each other's gaze, demonstrating a strong bluetooth connection and trust. Left to right: Muster Dog Pockets and Renee; Nathan and Muster Dog Chief.

STOCK SKILLS

When it comes to working stock, confidence is key. Encouraging the right level of confidence is a challenge.

Motivated by a desire to please you and driven by a natural desire to hunt, a well-bred and nurtured pup is likely to fly full throttle into the stock with a sense of invincibility. This can, of course, end in disaster for all involved, so a healthy level of caution is a necessary trait to encourage in your dog.

It's in these sessions where our trainers get their workout, leaping, diving and blocking their pup in an attempt to keep it at a safe and controllable distance off the stock without dampening its desire to herd.

This dynamic dance is frequently and best performed with a gliding rake.

PREPARING PUPPIES FOR PURPOSE

Muster Dog Chief learning to hold proper distance off his stock during a training session with Nathan.

THIS PAGE: With a steady and determined gaze, Muster Dog Pesto calmly works the chooks, showcasing her focused approach to work.

LEFT: Muster Dog Banjo impresses Kim as he backs the sheep with agility and enthusiasm.

BOTTOM LEFT AND RIGHT: Border collie Maggie May exhibits impressive eye and natural style while mastering sheep herding techniques.

TOP LEFT AND RIGHT: Five-month-old kelpie Busy Bee races to intercept a Brahman heifer breaking away from the mob, a massive feat for such a young pup.

PREPARING PUPPIES FOR PURPOSE 101

AWKWARD TEENAGERS

Full of attitude and sass, our puppies are now teenagers and literally falling over themselves to experience their world and everything working life has to offer. Like human teenagers, their hormones are in overdrive, and as the maturing dogs test the limits of their gangly growing bodies, they push boundaries that will also test your bond and influence over them.

LEFT: Muster Dogs Pockets is channelling her inner goofball, with her tongue out and eyes full of mischief.

PREPARING PUPPIES FOR PURPOSE

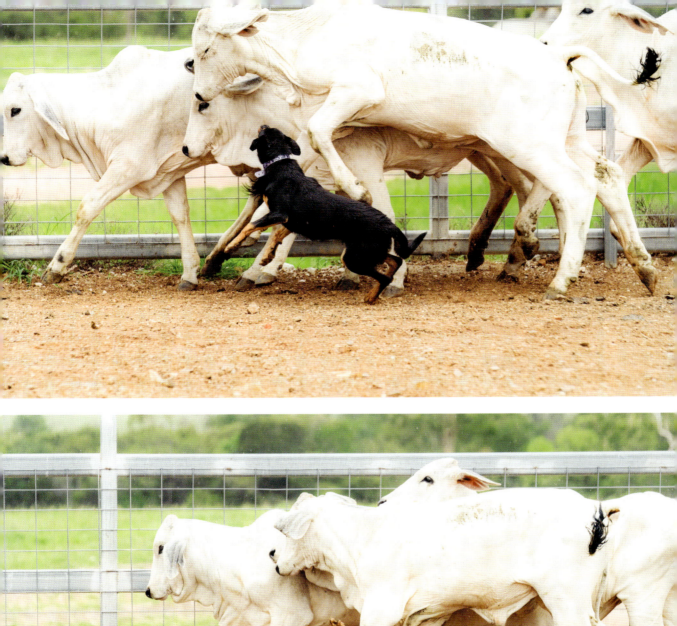

Muster Dog training isn't always smooth sailing. A teenage Muster Dog Annie stumbles during a training session on Brahman cattle.

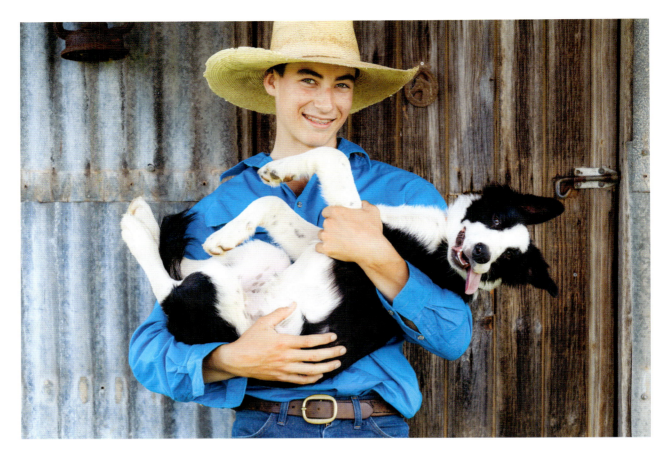

ABOVE: With a playful smirk, Muster Dog Chief hints at his spirited personality and joy for work.

RIGHT: Energetic and lively, Muster Dog Pesto is always on the go, eager to participate and contribute, adding vibrancy to every moment.

ABOVE: Kelpie Mighty reveals his playful side as Neil recalls him from the stock.

LEFT: Muster Dog Pockets, with a cheeky grin as she works the stock.

PREVIOUS PAGE: Kelpies Puff, Lulu and Soo work together as a team to block a beast that has broken away in the yards.

Muster dogs with good genes, and who have been nurtured and respectfully trained, live their best lives fulfilling their destiny as working dogs.

Witnessing the movement and prowess of working dogs is quite a marvel. Their agility and stamina are impressive, but it's the intimate display of intuition that takes your breath away. They pivot from poised anticipation to flying action in a dance of applied pressure and relief that creates a stir, a movement and ultimately the desired flow of stock across paddocks, into yards and onto trailers. This is what makes these dogs worth their weight in gold.

By twelve months of age, yesterday's pups are now dogs who have found their stride. They will have their preferred techniques, naturally drawing to the head of a herd or working the sides; reliably travelling over or back; and respecting you enough to stop, sit and stay as commanded. In rugged hills and cavernous valleys, they can be trusted to complete a blind cast, collect the mob and drive them to you at a pace that doesn't stress or split the stock, all while allowing mothers to travel with their calves or lambs and reach their destination with ease.

Some dogs will have more presence and get movement with little effort, others will need to use a bit of bark and hustle, but all of them should be effective members of the pack, ensuring safer, more efficient and enjoyable mustering than with machinery.

Muster dogs draw on their instincts, and the good ones will sense and see challenges before you do. With experience comes attitude, and like in all relationships, differing opinions will need to be overcome. They will make you laugh and swear, but they will never give up until the job is done.

CATTLE

A muster dog's bravery and ability to command beasts that could be more than fifty times their weight are skills not evident in any other hunter–prey relationship. The joy these dogs feel is evident in the sparkle in their eye as they stalk, bark and fly.

RIGHT: Muster dogs in action, rounding up the cattle with well-drilled teamwork.

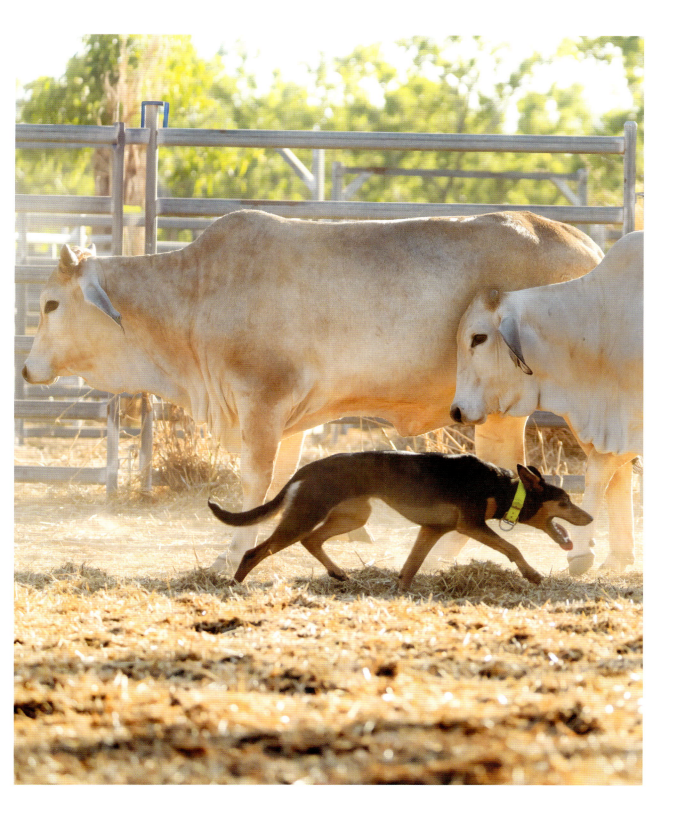

Our *Muster Dogs* handlers leading the way, with their loyal dogs alongside the stock. Top to bottom: Zoe; Nathan; and CJ.

RIGHT TOP AND BOTTOM: Muster Dog Ash and kelpie Axel go head-to-head with cattle at Joni Hall's dog school, showcasing determination and skill.

LEFT: Muster Dog Princess Annie holds her ground with regal confidence on the Brahman cattle.

LEFT: Muster Dog Spice shows pure curiosity and no fear in the face of a Brahman cow.

SHEEP AND GOATS

With their naturally flighty nature, sheep and goats offer thrilling challenges to muster dogs. Their size is less intimidating than that of cattle, and their leaps and springs make the mobbing-up more rigorous. They say sheep are followers, but a good working dog knows there is always a rebel in the flock, and if that dog is honest it's waiting for the break-away because the chase-down is invigorating and the reward the dog gets from its owner is always worth it.

RIGHT: Russ drafts sheep while his huntaways Chief and Rocky keep the stock moving.

BOTTOM RIGHT: The keen focus and determination in Muster Dog Ash's gaze signifies her relentless pursuit of excellence.

When working dogs are on their game, stock flow beautifully across country without any dreaded spills.

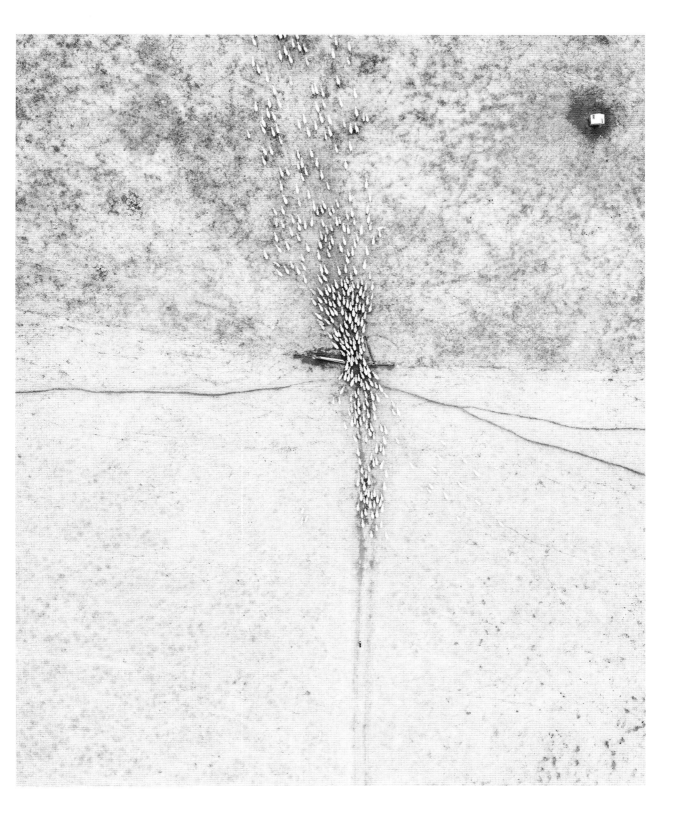

In the fading light of the sunset, Russ, the sheep and Muster Dog Molly head home; it's the end of another

WORKING WITH STYLE

Style is subjective, and a muster dog's working style is many things: sleek, poised, brave, discerning, clumsy or chaotic. While some traits and finesse are hereditary, it's the dog's personality that will define its unique working style and its best position in your pack.

RIGHT: Muster Dog Molly stylishly works in the sheep yards.

TOP LEFT: Kelpie Korra displays impressive style, kicking up a cloud of dust as she charges towards the stock.

BOTTOM LEFT: With a steady focus, border collie Hughie bends down and makes a slow, deliberate approach to the stock.

TOP RIGHT: Captured in motion, border collie Debbie's working style embodies grace, determination and the perfect balance of agility and focus.

BOTTOM RIGHT: Kelpie Puff's grin while stalking stock shows her joy for mustering.

The focused gaze and steadfast posture of these dogs are testament to their dedication in training. Kelpie Reggie (top left) keeps her eyes firmly fixed on the cattle as she dances around the mob. Muster Dog Snow (top far right) demonstrates sheer determination during the final assessment in series 2; his focused gaze and steadfast posture reveal his commitment to excelling in his training and proving his capabilities.

MATESHIP

True mateship is forged under trying conditions, where the work is tough, the terrain and weather are harsh and trust is essential. The relationship between a grazier and their dog is an unwavering bond. Their devotion and connection are enduring.

RIGHT: Russ with huntaway Chief, Muster Dog Molly and kelpie Ted, taking in the breathtaking mountain views in Bothwell, Tasmania.

The connection between Renee and kelpie Basalt transcends gravity as she carries him on her shoulder.

Muster Dog Buddy is perched up in the saddle with Zoe; his expression of contentment highlighting their special bond.

MUSTER DOGS IN ACTION

Moments of connection and closeness between dogs and their handlers are precious.

CLOCKWISE FROM RIGHT: Steve and Muster Dog Indi celebrate after their final assessment; Cilla enjoys a sunset with border collie Jackson, kelpie Axel and Muster Dog Ash; and Lily and Muster Dog Snow in matching blue.

Mick Hudson with Australian trial dog champion Rabbit.

Frank and his kelpies share a heartwarming bond. One of them affectionately wraps their paws around him in a big hug.

As the sun sets and another day draws to a close, our *Muster Dogs* champions Frank Finger (left) and Zoe Miller (right) are surrounded by their beloved dogs.

After the work is done, everybody looks forward to some playtime and cuddles.

RIGHT: Sidney's touch brings comfort to hardworking Muster Dog Ash; a moment of trust, companionship and innocence.

160   MUSTER DOGS

DOG TIRED

When the work's all done and it's knock-off time, the poised and stylish muster dogs let it all hang out to create a peaceful display of jiggly bits.

RIGHT: Four paws, one four-wheeler and a whole lot of cuteness! Kelpies Tango, Rio and Lorrie and Muster Dog Buddy, taking a well-earned rest in between jobs.

MUSTER DOGS

When not herding stock, kelpies and collies are always on the hunt for a sunny spot for a snooze.

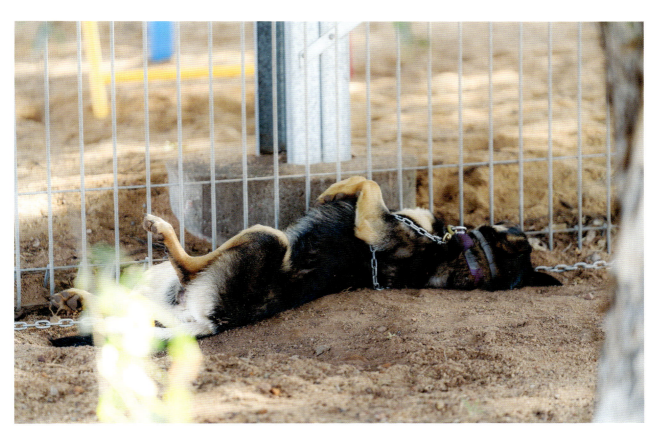

THIS PAGE: Kelpie Zelda takes relaxation to a new level, peacefully asleep with her legs in the air, embodying pure bliss and contentment. But when duty calls, she is all boundless energy once again.

MUSTER DOGS IN ACTION

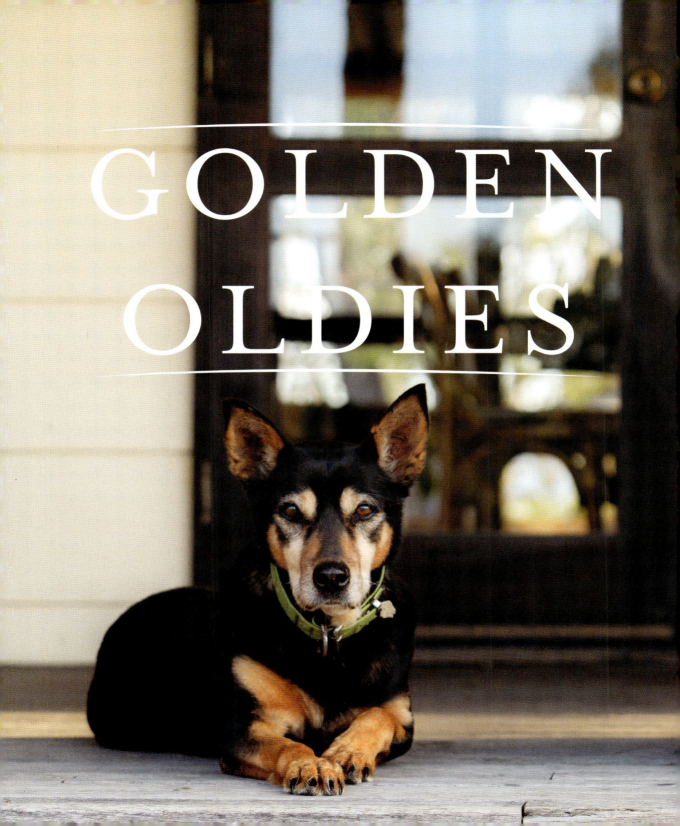

Full of wisdom and experience the old dogs know all the tricks. They've thrived in the good seasons and endured the bad ones. Their coats bear the scars of a useful working life. There is no beast, sheep or goat they can't contain, and they still have enough puff to chase down a clucking chook.

These muster dogs have earned the privileged spot on the veranda, yet they're always at the ready to be sent on that one last muster.

RIGHT: Retired dog Dude sits solemnly, gazing into the camera with a wise and weathered expression, reflecting a lifetime of loyalty and service.

MASTER AND APPRENTICE

With age comes experience, and with a quality bloodline comes instinct; the combination results in a reliable team leader. The elders balance the tempo of the pack, teaching the young pups patience and timing, how to conserve energy through dominance of eye, and how to obey commands with confidence and pride.

And when that elder is a pup's grandfather, aunt or cousin, the handler can be assured that the job will get done with the consistent coverage required.

GOLDEN OLDIES

Kelpie Tap enjoys the sunrise from the veranda, a well-earned reward for years of hard work.

ACKNOWLEDGEMENTS

Creating this book has been a labour of love, and it would not have been possible without the support, guidance and contributions of many wonderful people.

First and foremost, we would like to acknowledge the Traditional Owners of the Lands on which *Muster Dogs* was filmed and these images were taken.

Thank you to the participants, experts, graziers and their wonderful families who have opened their homes and hearts to us for this book and over the many years of filming *Muster Dogs*. Your stories and dedication have been the backbone of this series.

We would also like to pay tribute to the agriculture industry and the tireless efforts of farming families – both those with long associations to the land and those new to it – along with their remarkable working dogs.

In particular, we would like to express our gratitude to the breeders of the wonderful working dogs featured in *Muster Dogs* and this book. Special thanks to Joe Spicer for breeding the GoGetta working kelpies, Mick and Carolyn Hudson for breeding the MGH Australian working border collies, and Neil and Helen McDonald for breeding the Sherwood working kelpies.

A special thanks to our incredible crew and all those involved in the creation of the series and this book.

Thank you to the talented Melissa Spencer, whose work is featured in this book. Your skill and passion have truly captured the essence of our muster dogs.

Finally, to the readers, thank you for taking the time to explore these pages. It is our hope that these images and stories will inspire and move you, and connect you to the Australian agricultural industry and the wonderful world of muster dogs at work, at play and in moments of mischief and mateship.

LOCATIONS

Biggenden, Queensland: pp. 116–17, 120–21
Bothwell, Tasmania: pp. 132–33, 142–43, 150–51
Central Highland, Queensland: p. 123
Clermont, Queensland: pp. 130–31
Condamine, Queensland: pp. 122 (top), 126
Dunkeld, Victoria: p. 136
Keith, South Australia: pp. 20–21
Kingaroy, Queensland: pp. 6–7, 122 (middle), 129
Lillimur, Victoria: pp. 2–3, 87, 137

PHOTO CREDITS

All photographs © Stock Chick Films | Melissa Spencer, except for the following:

Ambience Entertainment / Brad Smith: p. 30 (top)

Ambience Entertainment / Ben Emery: pp. 16 (top), 28 (top and bottom left), 29 (top right)

Ambience Entertainment / Monica O'Brien: pp. 26–27, 30 (bottom), 181

Aticia Grey: pp. 12–13, 83 (top)

Jesse Smith: pp. 8, 15

ABOUT THE AUTHORS

Melissa Spencer

Melissa Spencer (Stock Chick Films) is a videographer/photographer and grazier from Capella, Queensland. With a working dog team of her own and years of experience working on cattle properties in Central Queensland, she has a deep passion for showcasing rural stories and the beauty and skill of Australia's working dogs through her lens. As a visual content creator specialising in video and photography of rural life and culture, she has also worked as a camera operator and photographer on the TV series *Muster Dogs*.

Monica O'Brien

Monica is an experienced creator and show runner across many genres including Factual Entertainment, Drama and Children's Entertainment. Over the past 17 years Monica has worked with Ambience Entertainment in production and development across a broad slate of programming, including *Magical Tales*, *Drop Dead Weird*, *Muster Dogs*, *Barrumbi Kids* and *The Garden Hustle*.

During her time writing, directing and producing the *Muster Dogs* series, Monica has travelled Australia meeting incredible people, learning about their communities and filming their beautiful dogs. Through that process she has been enriched by the stories of working dogs and the lives they live.

Michael Boughen

Michael Boughen has worked as an actor, writer, director and producer in the film and entertainment industry in the UK, Canada, New Zealand and Australia. He has written stage plays, TV drama, films and light-entertainment shows. A prolific producer, his credits include *Erky Perky*, *Figaro Pho* and major event TV such as MTV VMAs, Nickelodean Kid's Choice Awards and *Big Brother*. He produced the very first English-speaking version of *Deal or No Deal*.

He wrote and produced the feature film *Dying Breed* (2008), and produced Sean Byrne's *The Loved Ones* (2009), *Tomorrow, When the War Began* (2010), *Killer Elite* starring Jason Statham and Robert de Niro (2011), *Storm Boy* for Sony (2019) and *Interceptor* (2022), and wrote the feature *Great White* released in 2021. A prolific creator, he has created and written over 2000 hours of programming including the ABC hit *Muster Dogs*. He is currently producing Bruce Beresford's latest film *Overture*.

The ABC 'Wave' device is a trademark of the Australian Broadcasting Corporation and is used under licence by HarperCollins*Publishers* Australia.

HarperCollins*Publishers*
Australia • Brazil • Canada • France • Germany • Holland • India
Italy • Japan • Mexico • New Zealand • Poland • Spain • Sweden
Switzerland • United Kingdom • United States of America

HarperCollins acknowledges the Traditional Custodians of the lands upon which we live and work, and pays respect to Elders past and present.

First published on Gadigal Country in Australia in 2024
by HarperCollins*Publishers* Australia Pty Limited
ABN 36 009 913 517
harpercollins.com.au

Text copyright © Ambience Entertainment Pty Limited 2024

The right of Ambience Entertainment Pty Limited to be identified as the author of this work has been asserted by them in accordance with the *Copyright Amendment (Moral Rights) Act 2000*.

This work is copyright. Apart from any use as permitted under the *Copyright Act 1968*, no part may be reproduced, copied, scanned, stored in a retrieval system, recorded, or transmitted, in any form or by any means, without the prior written permission of the publisher. Without limiting the author's and publisher's exclusive rights, any unauthorised use of this publication to train generative artificial intelligence (AI) technologies is expressly prohibited.

A catalogue record for this book is available from the National Library of Australia.

ISBN 978 0 7333 4356 8

Edited by Brianna Street
Cover and internal design by Michelle Zaiter, HarperCollins Design Studio
Cover photographs © Stock Chick Films | Melissa Spencer
Colour reproduction by Splitting Image Colour Studio, Wantirna, Vic
Printed and bound in China by 1010 Printing on 128gsm matt art

6 5 4 3 2   25 26 27 28